Zipporah's Farm

by

Ani Perez

Illustrated by

Deborah Wilson

Lederer Children's Books
An imprint of
Messianic Jewish Publishers
Clarksville, MD 21029

This book is dedicated to my grandchildren

Liliana Grace, my #1. You are as sweet as you are beautiful.
You give me so much love and joy. You are the apple of my eye.
You have been a blessing to me and all who know you.

Melinda Isabella, whose innocent curiosity inspired me to write this book. You are so intelligent and funny. You amaze me.

Dean Luke, being my only grandson makes you unique.
I look forward to rough-housing with you.

Dylan Parker, I look forward to meeting you.
Still a newborn, grow and prosper. I will hold you in my arms soon.

I love you and pray blessings and well-being in every area of your lives.

Copyright 2018 © Ani Perez
Illustrations by Deborah Wilson

1 2018

ISBN Paperback: 978-1-936716-96-8
ISBN Hardcover: 978-1-936716-97-5

Messianic Children's Books
An imprint of Messianic Jewish Publishers
6120 Day Long Lane
Clarksville, MD 21029

Distributed by:
Messianic Jewish Publishers & Resources
Order line: (800) 410-7367
lederer@messianicjewish.net
www.MessianicJewish.net

Contents

Preface

Growing up in New York City, I never had much exposure to animals with the exception of dogs. My dog was always my best friend and, as a result, I learned how animals give unconditional love. The more I matured the more of an animal lover I became.

Three years ago I moved to a large farm in the country. I fell so in love with the cows, chickens and goats and had so much fun caring for them. Soon the wild animals started getting my attention. I would put food scraps onto a compost pile and watched the animals eat the various fruits and vegetable peelings and pits.

I noticed the animals were not afraid of me. They would run up to me and look at me as if they were studying me. I felt very much a part of the ecosystem.

I enjoyed watching them play, eat and interact with each other. There was a certain harmony that they lived in. The environment was that of peace and love. Soon I began to see the personalities of the different animals and gave them names accordingly.

The first one to get a name was Yael Chipmunk, with her two baby chipmunks. I would yell at her for chasing away the other animals from the food on the compost pile. She never stopped. Even some of the larger animals were afraid of her, especially Gideon Ground Hog.

Gideon was always so sweet. One time I found him eating my flowers and yelled at him. He never ate my flowers again. When I chased him out of my vegetable garden, he never went back in. He soon became my favorite animal friend.

Then there is Petra Possum, also one of my favorites. Petra only comes out at night. She is so shy! She would hide behind the maple tree and stare at me. Although all I could see were the shining of her two little eyes, I knew it was her. Little by little, she began to trust me and eventually started to go to the compost pile while I was still sitting outside. I saw such beauty in her. She seemed very gentle, yet strong. That is why I saw her as a former Israeli soldier.

Next there is Pinky the skunk. She would go into the hen house and eat the chicken's food. No matter how many times I chased her away, she would always be found in the feeding trough.

Whenever I saw Felix Red Fox, I knew the little animals where not safe. He may be pretty to look at but he could never be trusted.

David Bob Cat is strong and muscular. I never came face to face with David. I knew better. He would leave his huge paw prints all over my back yard. I could see he was a force to be reckoned with, so I put David, along with Petra in charge of protecting the smaller animals.

Isaiah Bald Eagle would fly over the farm, circling majestically as he appeared to float on air. What a sight to behold.

Ezekiel Wise Owl made his home in the maple tree in my backyard and would hoot as if complaining.

The squirrels are a lot of fun to watch. They are so playful. Chasing each other around as if they are playing a game of tag.

The flock of turkeys would roam around as if the farm were theirs. Every night they would roost in a different tree. That is for safety. They are pretty smart.

I would wake up every morning to the sounds of different birds. The crows are by far the loudest. The mourning doves the sweetest and the chickadees the quietist.

The farm is a migration stop for many types of birds. They would fly onto the hay field, eat up as many worms as they wanted, and then leave in the early morning hours. The sky would be covered with birds. It is a beautiful thing to see.

So you see, every animal mentioned in this book is real. I did talk to them but of course they did not talk back to me. I don't think they understand what I am saying. However, they hear my tone of voice and their instincts give them an understanding of my emotions.

I believe animals are a gift that God has given to us for our pleasure. They should be loved and protected. They are innocent and never should be killed for sport.

I welcome you to my farm, where there is an abundance of love, peace and joy. It is a place where anyone at any age can escape into fantasy and forget about the world's troubles, even if only for a little while. Welcome to Zipporah's Farm.

Ani Perez

About the Illustrator

Last fall, my husband and I went to Israel for the first time. I really didn't know what I would feel when I got there, and tried not to have any preconceived ideas. Among other things, I was surprised to find myself taking reference photos as though for a children's book. I had worked as an illustrator for many years, but had stopped illustrating about 10 years earlier in order to paint for galleries. So, I was very surprised to find that desire to do a children's book bubbling up within me while I walked through the Land.

When we returned home, I decided to contact various publishers. Soon afterwards, I received *Zipporah's Farm* in my emails for consideration. After years of illustrating for mainstream Christian publishers, I really desired to help produce literature that would be in line with my growth in my understanding of the Word. When I read Ani's story, I knew immediately that the Father had entrusted the artwork to me. It was perfect timing and the characters of the book walked in line with the Word. They celebrated the Sabbaths and the Festivals and served as examples of how we hope that our children and grandchildren will learn to walk. As I read the words of the story, I began to believe that the writer was lead by the Spirit in her choice of characters and events. Ani's characters came alive in my mind as I read the story, and I easily visualized how each one would appear. It was a labor of love for all who helped to make this book a reality.

I'm so thankful that Ani, Lisa Rubin of Messianic Jewish Publishers and I had the opportunity to work together on *Zipporah's Farm*. It was my joy to participate and I hope that it's a blessing to all who enter in.

Deborah Wilson

Zipporah's Farm

Autumn has fallen on Zipporah's farm. Summer's warm breeze has become fall's cool wind. The garden is growing gorgeously. The plants have gone into full bloom and are giving the most delicious fruits and vegetables. The pumpkin and squash patches are still flowering in all their glory, as a variety of mouthwatering treats grow according to ADONAI's timing. The tomato plants call out with their luscious fragrance. The corn stalks wave with their long leafy arms. The beans are ever searching for a place to expand, having found they put forth the most beautiful white flowers. The potato plants, however, are much more modest. They grow under the ground where they feel safe and warm. Potato flowers are a lovely lavender color with a bright orange dot growing out of the top. The leaves on the tree are excited about showing their true colors after being green since they budded. So proud, they argue about who will be yellow or red or orange. They can't wait to show their stuff.

The chickens realize the sun is going down sooner. They run into the safety of their little nested house at the first sign of sunset. Pinky, the skunk, sometimes goes into their house and eats their food when they are not looking. They squawk at the slightest little noise. The goats know their fur will grow to protect them from the cold. The little ones cannot wait to play in the snow. Momma and Poppa are not as happy about the snow as their kids are. The cows feel the same. Bertha would always moooan about how the

ground got colder every year as she got older. Martha, being much wiser, always had a happy thought about every season. She went on and on about all the good things that happen in the winter: "Well, the calves just love to lick the snowflakes as they fall from the sky." Martha also knew the part about autumn being the time of the High Holy Days. All the children and grandchildren would come for a visit. The children just loved all the animals on Zipporah's farm. Elias, the youngest bull on the farm loved to run and jump around whenever the children were visiting. It appeared to Zipporah that her little Elias was quite the performer. Nothing shy about him.

All the animals on the farm were *about their father's business*, as was Zipporah. The chimney attached to the wood stove had to be taken apart and cleaned. The wood had to be cut and stacked to put into the stove for heating and cooking. All the fruits and vegetables in the garden had to be harvested and canned. Just as we know we were created to give the Almighty His glory, the fruits and vegetables know that they were created to give us nutrition so that we would be healthy and have the strength to serve ADONAI.

The pumpkin washes nice and clean every day as Zipporah pours fresh water over her entire vine. She then lies in the heat of the sun, growing, hoping to make the award winning pumpkin pie. The tomatoes just know any spaghetti sauce made from them will be absolutely the best; they also are excellent in salads and in so many other ways. The celery, cabbage and broccoli have grown together in such a lovingly peaceful family. What a joy to behold. The pepper plants stand in a row, proud and tall like soldiers on guard. Under the ground the carrots, beets and ginger hope to be made into smoothies, while the onions and garlic share a bond of friendship.

The little animals are really starting to scurry now. Yael the Chipmunk, otherwise known to the little ones as Momma, runs to and fro collecting nuts, acorns, helicopters and anything else she can fit into her mouth. Zipporah is always happy to see Yael with a mouthful because that means two things: the first, Yael is about her Father's business, collecting food for herself and her children, Tamar and Yosef. Second, it means that with her mouth full of food she cannot yell at anyone, as she is known to sometimes do.

D'vora and Saul Squirrel are the sweetest young couple. They just got married this spring and hope to start a family soon. Zipporah's heart delights to watch the new Mr. and Mrs. Squirrel at play. They run so happily up and down the tree with an endless supply of energy. Gideon the Groundhog is one of Zipporah's special animal friends. Gideon is always alone. The other animals do not want to play with him. His oily fur leaves his scent behind, which no one can stand. The only friends Gideon has are the flies that follow him around and circle him. Gideon just loves to relax on a rock, basking in the rays of the sun. Mordechai the mole does not come out much. He has been blind since birth and can see nothing. He sometimes runs into Yael when the two of them are tunneling underground. That is not a pretty sight.

No farm would be complete without horses. Hal, the color of milk chocolate with a white diamond-shaped birthmark on his forehead, is humble and kind. In contrast, Rider, the most beautiful black retired racehorse, is proud and arrogant. Charger is curious and often wanders off the farm on his own.

There are so many different types of birds on the farm. Some stay year round, like Blue jay, Chickadee and Crow. Others only come for the summer, while others come for an overnight visit. You see, many birds migrate north in the summer and south in the winter. Each flock of birds that passes this way absolutely looks forward to the visit twice a year. Zipporah loves to welcome all creation to the farm and share all the wonderful blessings our generous Creator has given us.

Luke and Hanna Turtle-Dove make their appearance for every celebration. Always elegant, they gracefully glide to a tree branch especially chosen for having just the right amount of covering to allow them to see as well as be seen, yet remain discrete. Sometimes, a couple or three leaves would huddle together in just the right way as to allow the perfect amount of privacy for Luke to feel comfortable enough to lean in and give Hanna a little peck on the cheek. Any tree would be honored to host such a devoted couple. Even with a celebration in full swing, they only have eyes for each other, content to romantically coo back and forth.

Let us not forget Isaiah Bald Eagle, wise and majestic. Isaiah appears to float across the sky so magnificently. Zipporah is so amazed by Isaiah's meek and humble manners. Always soft spoken, Isaiah need not ever raise his voice. So strong and mighty, he feels no need to ever display the fullness of his strength. So highly respected, not only birds, but everyone on Zipporah's farm loves to sit around and listen to Isaiah teach ADONAI's word for hours on end. No one could ever get enough of what he had to say. Always loving, never harsh, Isaiah could debate scriptures with the best of rabbis. None can surpass him in wisdom, although Ezekiel Wise

Owl comes very close. Ezekiel is more worldly wise, whereas, Isaiah gets his wisdom from the Word of Adonai. "Adonai's word is final," he liked to say when he and Ezekiel would go back and forth about life's unanswerable questions.

The deer have gone into hiding. It is hunting season. As Zipporah ponders this, the turkeys have not been around as often. Maybe they're also hiding from the hunters.

All the animals know that Zipporah's farm is a sanctuary where hunters are not welcome and the animals are free and safe as long as they are within the borders of the farm. Zipporah's farm is so welcoming that anyone with the love of Adonai in their hearts wants to come, and then don't want to leave. Although they know they must leave, they all know they will be coming back and look forward to the events throughout the year. There are many celebrations like Purim and Shavuot, biblical holidays that Adonai gave to His people to enjoy.

Sometimes Zipporah has to protect the little animals from the bigger, hungrier animals that want to eat them.

David the Bobcat is the best predator because he is patient and quiet. He knows when it is time to be still and wait on Adonai and just when to move in and let instinct take over. David has a gentle spirit. He understands Gd's chain of command. He knows he can be eaten. Just as he eats. The difference is that David loves Adonai and obeys and relies on His grace. He always leaves a tenth of what he has to eat for the smaller weaker animals. David knows God's Word says to feed and care for the widows and fatherless, the less fortunate.

David is mighty and strong, a protector of the weak. One could see his toned muscles under the most spectacular coat of fur. David is loved by many. The smaller animals run to greet him as soon as he makes his appearance. He often comes with gifts.

The Coyotes are different. They have no reverence for Abba, Father, or love for His creation. They travel in packs and seek out innocent animals smaller than themselves. They all gang up together and are not kind at all. That is why they are never welcome on the farm. Zipporah must always keep a watchful eye out for her little furry friends who are no match for a hungry pack.

Felix Red Fox often wanders over from Fox Forest, where he lives with other red, silver, and the rare and ever elusive, blue foxes. Zipporah often gets concerned when Felix lets out his toothy grin and looks up at her with those sly eyes. She senses a certain uneasiness whenever he is on the farm and finds herself looking for the smaller animals, even if only to put her own mind to rest.

So, there you have it in a nutshell: one little acre of land given to provide and protect. A place where Adonai is always welcome. Where grace, peace, joy and love are abundant. All members of one family, Adonai's Family.

Gideon's Bad Day Turns Good

As Gideon awoke from a deep, restful sleep, he whispered the same words he had every morning since Momma groundhog first taught him these words, "Boker Tov, ABBA." Gideon always started his day by saying "Good Morning" to his heavenly "DADDY." He spoke ever so softly. Gideon would imagine "The Throne Room." ABBA, Yeshua and Ruach, along with all the Angels, and Elders. Remembering the Heroes of Scripture.

Gideon has so much love in his heart but no one to give it to. He doesn't have any friends or family. Gideon thinks about his Momma and wishes she was here with him, but all animals after a certain age must take care of themselves. With this being Gideon's first summer on his own, he hasn't made any friends yet. He often watches the animal families at play, but Gideon hasn't any family or even someone to talk to.

Gideon hoped this day would be different. It was a very special day because it was his birthday. Before he left the comfort of his little bed, he whispered one last prayer request, "ABBA, Please let me find a friend today. I don't want to be alone anymore." As Gideon made his way through the dark underground tunnel, before reaching the surface of the ground he reminded himself, "If you want to have a friend you have to be a friend."

When Gideon finally reached ground level he first stuck his little head out looking all around in order to be safe. When he felt secure enough, he jumped right out of his hole and was off to breakfast. As Gideon sat happily eating his birthday breakfast he saw Tamar and Yosef at play. Gideon called over, "May I play too"? The two little chipmunks looked at each other, not knowing what to say so they said nothing. Of course, Gideon thought they didn't hear him. He was off, running toward them so happy to have found someone to play with, he could hardly contain himself. "Hey you two, guess what. Today is my birth…" By the time Gideon got to the twins they were almost in a panic. They knew what would happen if Momma found them playing with Gideon, or Stinky, as Momma liked to call him. It was too late, Momma had been watching and saw and heard everything from the woodpile. Yael was already en route to intercept. She speedily jumped into one of her many entrance holes and started tunneling to rescue her children.

Yael popped out of the ground right in front of her little ones, as if to protect them, "Stay away from my babies, you stinky thing!" She then reached out her tiny hand and grabbed Dvora and Yosef by their even tinier hands and rushed them home yelling about how she would need to scrub them clean. The pair could only look at each other knowingly.

Gideon was left standing there wondering what happened. Sadness came over him as he realized the children were not allowed to play with him, but did not understand why. He thought for a moment, I love ADONAI and His creation, I pray, I try to obey ADONAI the best I can, so, why are the twins not allowed to play with me. Gideon did not have an answer. Overwhelmed with sadness, Gideon tried to swallow the lump in his throat and fight back the tears. Being the brave soul that he was, he decided to pray for Yael and the twins.

After praying, Gideon set out to have fun on his birthday.

"PINKY!!!!" Gideon ran toward the skunk, calling out her name.

"What," Pinky yelled back, "Why are you shouting my name?"

"Do you want to play with me? Today is my birthday, you know."

"No."

Gideon stopped mid-step, "NO? You didn't know it was my birthday?"

"I had no idea and frankly, I really don't care. I have a birthday of my own. Why would I care about yours?"

Gideon's heart stopped. He felt like he had been punched in the chest. He could not catch his breath. His mind was going in different directions trying to understand why Pinky would say something so mean.

When Gideon was finally able to form a thought he simply asked, "Why are you being so mean to me?" That was all he could say? With tears running down his plump little check, his head hung low, unable to look her in the eyes. At that moment, he just wanted to be invisible so no one could see the depth of his pain.

His hurt was so deep that it was all he could feel. Suddenly Gideon let out such a cry from all that was within him. The sound echoed in the valley reaching Zipporah. Her heart was so filled with compassion that she fell to her knees. Feeling Gideon's pain, Zipporah asked ADONAI what she could do to help Gideon. The answer came quick and simple, "LOVE HIM." A smile came across Zipporah's face. "This is easy because I do love him." Zipporah thanked ADONAI for such a quick answer to her simple prayer. Knowing what needed to be done, Zipporah got up off her knees and went right to work.

Gideon had no idea how much time had passed or even where he was. Overcome with grief, he barely had the strength to keep on walking or even lift his head. His feet felt heavy as he dragged them over the meadow. He could not think of a time when he had ever felt so alone. He could not understand why no one wanted to play with him.

Because tears blurred his eyes, he did not see them coming and was unaware of any danger until he heard the first voice.

"Well, hello there," he heard in a voice that was not familiar to him. As he wiped his eyes he could see the pack of three coyotes as they licked their chops.

Gideon did not have time to think. He knew it was the end for him.

Before Gideon could say a word, a familiar voice rang through the valley, "DON'T YOU DARE TOUCH HIM!" Zipporah shouted as she rode toward the pack on Hal Horse's back with David Bobcat at her side and Isaiah Bald Eagle flying overhead. The coyotes new they were in trouble so they just turned and ran off without another word.

"Gideon, we have been looking all over for you. Where have you been?" she asked as she finally caught up to him. And David the Bobcat scooped Gideon onto his back as if he was one of his own cubs.

"Me? You…looking…for me? Why?" Gideon appeared confused.

"It's your birthday, silly. Everyone is waiting on the farm to start your birthday party."

"Me? My party?" Gideon repeated her words in unbelief.

"Yes, we have cake and ice cream and presents." Zipporah could barely contain her excitement.

"Cake? Ice cream? For me?"

"Of course for you," Zipporah reassured him, "Who else has a birthday today?"

Zipporah gave Gideon a kiss on the forehead. He felt like a giant as he rode on David's muscular back all the way to the farm where everyone was waiting to wish him a happy birthday and get the party started.

Pinky was the first to greet him. Jumping up and down with excitement, "Happy Birthday, Gideon. I'm sorry I was mean to you earlier today. Can you forgive me?" Pinky could talk faster than most people could think.

"Of course, I forgive you. It has already been forgotten," Gideon said, his eyes widened with surprise to see how many new friends he now had. "Well, let us give thanks and then have some cake and ice cream." Gideon's heart, so filled with love, now overflowed to all around him.

"Don't forget the presents," Pinky said feeling like she would explode if all those secret little treasures weren't revealed that very moment. "There are so many of them. What do you think are in all the pretty packages? Let's count then. Wow look at this one. Can you open this one first?"

Zipporah's smile widened as she thought of an idea to quiet Pinky down. She lovingly walked over and handed Pinky one of the decorative plates with a huge slice of the yummiest looking cake Pinky had ever seen, covered in her favorite kind of ice cream.

"Thank you Zipporah. How did you know pistachio is my favorite? It goes with chocolate. Those two are the best. This is great. What a day. Did you know my birthday is in the spring? Will we have a party like this for my birthday?"

Realizing her plan failed, Zipporah bent down to Pinky's level and put her hand on Pinky's little cheek and said, "Pinky, I love and treat all my friends equally. Therefore, yes we will have a party for you but not like this one. This is a Gideon party, like for a boy. You will have a Pinky party. Much more colorful and planned according to YOUR personality." Zipporah gave Pinky a kiss on that cute little cheek. As she did, Zipporah softly whispered into Pinky's tiny ear, "Young ladies chew with their mouths closed."

Pinky's face turned the most adorable shade of red as she shrugged her shoulders and quietly shoved another spoonful into her mouth, savoring the treat.

Satisfied with her final results Zipporah was off to celebrate with Gideon. "Happy Birthday, my dear." She so loved this little critter. "What a wonderful day for a party."

Gideon felt so loved at that moment. He looked his guardian in the eyes and smiled. "Zipporah," Gideon said, filled with more good emotions than he could express, "Thank you. No one has ever given me a party before."

"Well, then, this is your first, but as long as you live on the farm, it will not be your last." Zipporah reassured him in a way that he knew was sincere.

At a loss for words, Gideon shyly stood there next to someone very special to him, who knows he is equally special. It suddenly dawned on Gideon and he shared his thought with Zipporah.

"This morning I was sad because I had no friends and now I have more friends than I can count. I am so happy. I feel like a new groundhog."

"Gideon, we have always been here and will be as long as Adonai gives us life. We are all family here on the farm, don't you ever forget that. You can always come to me whenever you need a friend."

Gideon knew Zipporah meant what she said, for she would never lie.

That night, while Gideon was saying his bedtime prayers, he gave a special thanks to his Abba. Sharing such an awesome time, Gideon knew he would never be the same.

So, this is how Gideon's bad day turned good. With the help of a few obedient servants, Adonai was able to show Gideon how much He loved him, everyone on the farm loved him and no one is ever forgotten by his Creator, especially on their birthday.

Yael Must Learn to Share

Zipporah's Farm is known near and far for its compost pile. Whenever Zipporah would peel fruit or vegetables she would always leave a little extra for her little animal friends. Summer is the best. Zipporah would cut the tops off of pineapples leaving plenty of sweet, juicy fruit for the sharing. The mango pits are Yael Chipmunk's favorite, with so much extra mango on the already delicious seed. Yael and her twins, Tamar and Yosef, often enjoyed digging through the compost pile in search of nutritious treats. The only problem is that Yael thought the compost was all for her. The truth is, Zipporah wanted all her little furry friends to eat well and enjoy. Yael would have none of that. Those goodies were for her and her babies, to hear Yael tell it.

One day as Zipporah was in the cabin washing dishes she heard that all too familiar screech and knew who it was. "Yael," Zipporah called out to her, "What is the matter?"

Yael lifted her tiny head and proceeded to tell Zipporah how she did not want Gideon eating her food.

"Gideon?" Zipporah knew Gideon is honest and obedient. She gave him the chance to defend himself.

"Well… I… I thought….um…" Gideon did not know what to say. He did not think he was doing anything wrong…and he wasn't. He only wanted to have a snack. He knew the compost was for everyone. So what had he done wrong?

"Would someone please tell me what is going on?" Zipporah had an idea by now but waited to hear from the source.

"He cannot just waddle over here and help himself to whatever he wants," Yael jeered.

"And may I ask why not?" Zipporah knew she had to defend Gideon.

"Because, this is *my* compost and he can't have any." Yael seemed so sure of herself.

"Is that a fact?" Zipporah replied.

"Yes it is and this conversion is getting old!" Yael not only folded her little arms but she also rolled her eyes and stuck her nose in the air.

Zipporah almost laughed at the sight of this four-inch chipmunk's defiance, but thought better and simply asked, "When did all this God-given food become yours?"

"Well," Yael said, showing such indignation, "I have been eating here since my Momma built her nest and taught me how to gather for supper."

"That may be true," Zipporah said with all the patience she could muster. "However, other animals have lived here before you were ever born. Does that give them the right to tell you, *you* cannot eat here?"

"I wish they would try and see what they get!" Yael was now losing her temper.

"Allow Gideon to eat from the compost that Adonai has given to all the animals on the farm to be eaten freely. No ifs, ands or buts about it." Zipporah was stern but loving as she turned and went back to her cabin. Can you imagine the nerve of that little Momma? She must learn to share.

Yael knew she lost this round but the fight was far from over, in her eyes.

One day after walking for miles over the summer after hearing about Zipporah's Farm, an old gray squirrel by the name of Methuselah finally could see in the distance, grass greener than the emerald Isles themselves.

He just knew that had to be the place of his dreams. Suddenly, Methuselah felt younger and stronger as he began a full trot onto Zipporah's Farm.

The smell of the grass and hay were heavenly to Methuselah. He hadn't realized how hungry he was until that moment. Traveling all day with nothing to eat, he started to feel faint. Methuselah helped himself to a few acorns and was so content to be in such a lovely place. He wandered around looking for someone who lived here. Before he knew where he was he could smell the most delicious aromas. Suddenly he realized, this must be the famous compost pile he had heard so such about.

The stories didn't even come close to the real smell and taste of the nutritious treats he found. Nibbling happily on a piece of carrot, Methuselah smiled as he thanked his Heavenly father for such a treat.

Suddenly there came a loud screech. "Who are you and what are you doing eating my food?"

"So sorry, my lady, I thought this was Zipporah's Farm."

"It is," Yael yelled. "My question remains, who are you?"

"Allow me to introduce myself," said Methuselah.

"I don't care what your name is; just get out of my food pile."

Methuselah was confused. He had been told that the compost pile on Zipporah's Farm was for everyone, free for the taking. "Let me explain."

"No explanation needed. Just leave." Yael stood her ground.

As Methuselah was stepping off the pile of delightful treats, he sadly apologized.

"Yael that is not how we treat newcomers to the farm." Zipporah came to Methuselah's rescue.

Methuselah knew instinctively who was speaking. "You must be Lady Zipporah"? He asked as he respectfully bowed.

"Just Zipporah." She smiled graciously. "Please help yourself to something to eat. Has your journey been a long one?"

"Too long, my lady." Methuselah answered still bent at the waist. "I am faint with hunger and exhaustion."

"You are welcome here." Zipporah said, talking more to Yael than Methuselah. "You may stay as long as you like and have anything you want to eat. This is your home now."

Still a bit shaken up by Yael, Methuselah needed reassurance, "This lady has said the food in this pile belongs to her and I may not have any."

"In time, you will get used to Yael," Zipporah warned Methuselah. "She yells at everyone and most don't pay any attention to her. After you've eaten and gotten enough rest I will show you around and introduce you to your new family. I'm sure Dvora and Saul Squirrel would just love to make your acquaintance. They are a lovely young couple. Everyone on the farm is friendly and welcoming," Zipporah reassured Methuselah. "Yael takes her motherly instincts just a little too far." The two of them laughed together for the first time and at that very moment Methuselah knew he had found a home.

With that, Methuselah happily filled his belly and went down for a mid-day nap.

Yael's ever watchful eyes were fixed on the twins as she sat on "her rock," at the top of the compost pile.

As the twins sat munching on a bedtime snack, Tamar saw her first. She looked up from her feast to see the most beautiful set of eyes looking up at her. "Shalom," Tamar said welcoming a new family member, as she liked to call the other farm animals. Petra's classic beauty was stunning. "Have you come to share a snack with us?" Tamar, unlike her Mom, enjoyed the company of other animals. Yael was still observing the whole scene from where she stood guarding the only two lives she cared anything about.

By this time, Yosef sat staring at the most perfectly triangular shaped face he had ever seen. Unable to find the right words, Yosef tried to speak but the words refused to leave his brain and travel out of his mouth. "Oh, um, my um….."

Petra smiled as she introduced herself. "My name is Petra Possum. What might your names be?" She asked gazing at the most adorable set of twins she had ever seen in all of her life.

"My um…um" was all Yosef could say.

"I think he is trying to say his name is Yosef." Tamar helped her brother, not knowing what had gotten into him. "Tamar is mine."

"Try some of these beets. Zipporah says beets are good for your blood."

"Thank you," Petra said, gracefully making her way up the compost pile. Petra did not walk; she sort of sauntered as one who hadn't a care in the world. She politely curtsied.

That was as much as Yael could take. She prepared to move into action. Petra was reaching out her dainty little hand to lovingly stroke the twins on the cheek. With that, Yael pounced from guard duty on her favorite rock straight through the air and landed right in front of Petra, pushing her onto her back.

Petra looked up in amazement. She had never been attacked like that before but knew just what to do. She called out to ADONAI her protector. Petra knows her ADONAI would always protect her, no matter what.

Petra saw Yael was about to strike her again. In what seemed to be seconds, Petra whispered a quiet prayer: "Father, please forgive me for what I am about to do." Petra having never been in a brawl was hoping to avoid defending herself. "Please, I mean no harm." She tried to talk her way out of the uncomfortable situation in a lady-like manner, but Yael would have none of that. Yael balled up her comically tiny fist, her teeth clenched in rage as she fixed her glaring eyes at Petra and charged forward. Swinging wildly, Yael thought she was going to punch Petra's lights out.

One thing Yael did not know was that Petra had been a member of the Israeli Defense Force, the IDF. Highly trained, Petra knew she should only defend herself and never attack first.

In an attempt to defend herself, Petra put out her hand and Yael ran into it nose first. Landing flat on her back, laying where she fell, Yael could not believe what just happened. Dazed by the blood running down her face more than the impact itself.

The sound of her baby's screams brought Yael back to her awareness of the potential danger.

"PLEASE DON'T HURT OUR MOMMA!!!!!" They pleaded in unison.

Zipporah was so caught up in delightful worship, she hadn't heard anything before the twins screamed. Alarm ran through her as she prayerfully rushed to the defense of her "little Momma."

Petra, filled with equal amounts of remorse and empathy, attempted to comfort the children. "Forgive me, I didn't want to hurt her. I don't like hurting people. You never need to be afraid of me."

By the time Zipporah arrived, Petra was helping Yael stand up. Still unsteady on her feet, her pride was hurt more than anything. Tamar and Yosef clung to their Momma's skinny little legs, which, about now felt as elastic as rubber bands.

"I'm sure there must be a perfectly good explanation for what I see before me," Zipporah announced. Somehow she knew Yael would be at the heart of it, but decided to give her the benefit of the doubt.

"This animal assaulted me." Yael managed to appear wounded.

"I was defending myself. This would not have happened had she not felt the need to be so aggressive. This "hit first, ask questions later," behavior is not wise. Think of your children. Is there a lesson to be learned here?"

"The young lady is right." Ezekiel Owl had been watching from a tree, finding the whole thing quite entertaining.

"Although, it was fun watching Yael get what she long had coming to her," he could not help teasing the newly humiliated Momma. "Children do follow the example of their parents. It is surprising how well behaved your children are."

"Ezekiel," Zipporah turned everyone's attention back to the matter at hand. "If you choose to speak of examples you must be willing to show good, in word as well as deed. If you have nothing good to say, perhaps, you should not say anything at all."

Ezekiel, feeling indignant, replied in his usual haughty manner. "I am not the one pursuing violence."

"We will have none of that here." Zipporah was now filled with righteous indignation. "This farm is a sanctuary for anyone who wants to live peacefully; all others are not welcome."

"Yael, it is time for you to make a choice." Zipporah put forth her ultimatum, "You may stay on the farm only if you show more "fruit of the Spirit"— self-control, love, joy, peace, longsuffering, kindness, faithfulness and gentleness."

Yael sensed the seriousness in Zipporah's tone.

"If you can't live by the fruit of the Spirit, you must go. Your children may stay. They will be well cared for."

Panic went through Yael like a tidal wave, "No, please. I will show good fruit. I cannot live without my babies."

So, that is how Yael learned to share. She never again chased anyone off the compost pile

Petra Possum and Yael Chipmunk ended up becoming very dear friends. Yael knew no one would ever be a better baby-sitter for the twins than Auntie Petra. Of course, the twins just loved being around Petra. She is one of the most good-natured critters one could ever meet. That is why, to know her is to love her. Even the other animals on the farm say Petra is having a good effect on Yael. They are less afraid of her and they eat better as a result. So, all is well that ends well.

Hanukkah on the Farm

The view outside the bay window of Zipporah's bedroom is a sight to behold. In the distance the sun peaks out from behind the mountain announcing the new day. The sky lights up in the most spectacular shades of mauve, lavender and blue. The trees in the foreground appear almost as tall as the backdrop of the mountains, complementing each other as only nature can. The hayfield between the tree line that borders Zipporah's Farm is not just beautiful, but also serves to feed and house the animals and birds.

Zipporah rubbed the sleep out of her eyes in order to take in the fullness of the complete eco-system before her. "*Baruch Elohaynu*, Blessed be our Lord. *Atah Hu Malkeinu*, You are our King. *Todah l'Mosheeaynu*, Thank you our Messiah." Zipporah loved starting her day by putting God in His rightful place. "Praise Him in the morning, thank Him at night," she would say. She knew very well that time with her savior is always the best way to start the day. "If you start your day with prayer, thanksgiving and praise, everything else will fall into place," was her motto.

Zipporah spent extra time with God that morning because it was *Shabbat*, the Sabbath, which is her much needed day of rest. This Sabbath was even more special because sundown will begin Day 1 of *Hanukkah*, the Festival of Dedication, an 8-day commemoration of the re-dedication of the Temple in Jerusalem.

There once was a very evil and arrogant king by the name of Antiochus Epiphanes. He sent men to attack the holy city of Jerusalem. They destroyed the city, burned property, shed much innocent blood in the Temple, took woman and children captive and took their animals. As if that weren't bad enough, he went into the Temple and took all the treasures from the Sanctuary. This king was so bad that he sacrificed unclean animals on God's Holy Altar.

He made bad laws and forced some of the children of Israel to renounce Adonai. Soon many people, Gentiles and Jews, worshipped pagan gods and burned sacrifices to false idols.

One man named Judah Maccabee, called "The Hammer," led ordinary men to battle against this terrible king's army. These brave men went to war to protect the God-given right of the children of Israel to worship the one true God. Some say Judah Maccabee won the war but his obedience to God was what enabled them to prevail. We need to remember that God rewards those who trust and obey him.

Once the war was won the first order of business was to cleanse and rededicate the Temple using the Golden Lampstand and the special oil. But only one solitary bottle of prepared oil was found, only enough to give light for one day. By a miracle of God that one bottle of oil lasted eight days. That's why we light the Hanukkah menorah, the *Hanukkiah*, for eight days. That is why Hanukkah is sometimes known as "the Festival of Lights" or "the Festival of Dedication."

Zipporah stood in the back yard looking for the three stars that would signify the end of Sabbath. The only difference is tonight, instead of lighting a Havdalah candle, to close the Sabbath, she will light the first Hanukkah candle of this season. Zipporah smiled when she saw Petra shyly peeking at her from the perfect vantage point between a rock and a maple tree. Petra Possum smiled back warmly as her eyes radiated in the dark and ran to Zipporah's side, thrilled to spend her first Hanukkah on the farm. "Is it time yet?!?!" Petra's normal cool, calm and collected behavior gave way to excitement far beyond anything she had ever experienced.

"One, Two, Three. Yes, sweetie; it is time. Would you like to watch from the window as I light the candles?"

"WAIT. Don't start without us." Yael could be heard a mile away. "Hurry," she yelled to Tamar and Yosef. "Zipporah cannot delay all evening for you."

"We're coming, Momma." Yosef arrived before his twin sister, Tamar, who made her appearance only seconds later.

Soon Gideon Groundhog, David Bobcat and Pinky Skunk showed up as other animals and birds found a spot with a view of the dining room table, where Zipporah kindled the lights of the menorah every year.

Zipporah put on one of her favorite head coverings and lit the *shamash*, the "servant" candle, as she did every evening during Hanukkah.

"Blessed are You, Lord our God, King of the universe, who has sanctified us by your commandments and instructed us to kindle the lights of Hanukkah."

"Blessed are You, Lord our God, King of the universe, who has performed miracles for our ancestors in days of old at this season."

"Blessed are You Lord our God, King of the universe, who has kept us in life, preserved us, and enabled us to reach this season."

"Let the celebration begin!"

Zipporah went right to work in the kitchen. Shredding the potatoes for the *latkes*, potato pancakes. Of course they have to be served with sour cream or applesauce. She also fried up Israeli apple fritters.

The compost pile that feeds the animals was filled with all kinds of fruits and vegetables, enough to go around for the celebration. Everyone danced and sang. Some played *dreidel*, spinning the top, while others watched and cheered on. Elias Bull is always the life of the party, running and jumping around. Pinky will talk to anyone who would listen, whereas Petra enjoys sitting back and taking it all in. The Twins absolutely love being around Petra. They feel safe with her being IDF and all. David Bobcat is ever watchful for unwelcomed intruders who may want to harm one of the smaller animals. David Bobcat saw Felix Red Fox enter the farm and decided to be the first to greet him.

"Shalom, Felix," David offered peace, but never let down his guard.

"Happy Hanukkah. Nice to see you David," Felix spoke ever so softly, almost a sly whisper.

"You had better mind your manners," David warned sternly. "If even one of those little ones goes missing you will be supper for day two of Hanukkah."

"Why, David, you know how much I love the little ones." His toothy grin gave his thoughts away.

"Yes I do." David, much wiser than Felix, was not going to fall for his play on words. "You, on the other hand would be chewy and not as tender."

Felix knows David is a force to be reckoned with. "You have such a sense of humor," he said as he tried not to show just how afraid he really was.

"I'll be watching you," was David's last warning.

Gifts, food and laughter are the theme of this night. Love is the greatest gift shared on these 8 nights. Everyone gives of himself for the betterment of the farm. All live in harmony year round but celebrations are always heavenly. A blanket of white snow as far as the eye can see and the colorful flames from the bon-fire kept everyone warm and cozy.

"Please don't get too close; safety first." Zipporah cared for her little furry friends. "Come let us huddle together for warmth." She just loved when the animals sat on her lap or shoulders.

At this time Zipporah stood to open in prayer.

"Lord, Mighty God, Most High, Great, awesome God, may You who makes peace for us, make peace for all Israel, and say Amen. God, thank You very much for this celebration. You are welcome as God and Ruler because You made us for Your good pleasure. May we be pleasing to You this evening and always. In the name of Yeshua the Messiah, and everyone say, Amen."

"AMEN!!!!!!!!!!!!" rang throughout the valley and could be heard by anyone whose heart was open to the Ruach Ha Kodesh, the Holy Spirit of God. The Anointing of God fell upon all in attendance.

"At this point I would like to turn the festivities over to Isaiah Bald Eagle. I cannot think of anyone wiser to lead us in God's Word." Embarrassed by the statement, Ezekiel Wise Owl took exception to the comment, rolling his large eyes.

With that, all the animals and birds found their place and settled down giving Isaiah full attention. Zipporah went inside her cabin to listen from the window, allowing sleep to peacefully come.

Preparation for Day 2 of Hanukkah was very busy for Zipporah. She could hardly contain herself. All the animals knew someone special was coming: Micah, a K-9 companion to an Israeli Defense Force soldier. Micah has the shiniest black coat of fur anyone has ever seen. He is a gentle giant, so full of love and more playful than most of the other animals.

Zipporah knows how important hospitality is. She is also a patriot. "We must pray for our soldiers every day and help whenever and wherever we can." She would say, "These soldiers are *mishpochah*, family. A good meal in a family environment is essential for the morale of good men and woman who serve and protect. Even if it causes them to lose

their lives, they know God will bring them home to himself. The brave sacrifices they make are repaid, sometimes in this life, other times in the next."

The knock on the door brought Zipporah back from her thoughts. Micah plowed his way in looking for a treat.

"Please come in." Zipporah was happy to see the young handsome soldier who stood at the door.

The animals scurried for a spot at the window to see the brave soldier they knew so little about. They were proud of him. David Bobcat was the first to speak: "You see that soldier? It is because of him that we have freedom, DO NOT ever forget that. We must show respect. The K-9 who is with him is one of us and could be any of us. Let us lift them up in prayer." David had the courage of many K-9 soldiers, yet he was always gentle and kind to all who needed protection.

Leading up to day two of Hanukah was very busy for Zipporah. She could hardly contain herself. All the animals knew someone special was coming. Zipporah knows how important it is to show hospitality.

These families are *mishpochah*. A good meal in a family environment is essential for fellowship. The knock on the door brought Zipporah back from her thoughts. "Please come in." Zipporah was happy to see the young father who stood at the door with his daughter. The animals scurried for a spot at the window to see the little girl and her dad they knew so little about. They were proud of him. David Bobcat was the first to speak. "We must show respect. The family unit is so important. This child lost her mother before she was old enough to remember her."

"That little girl doesn't know who her Momma is?" Tamar asked

"Well," Isaiah thought for a moment, "she has seen pictures of her Momma, so she knows what she looks like. But she is not able to give her a hug or talk to her. That's why it is so important that young women like Zipporah take an interest in young girls like Esther. Be an example of a woman of God. Show her how to follow God from a woman's point of view."

"Let us lift them up in prayer." David had the courage of many, yet he was always gentle and kind to all who needed protection.

Zipporah kindled Day 2 candles and the celebration started all over again. The cabin's aroma was that of a bakery since Zipporah ended each meal with a sweet, fruity, nutty confection. Compost had been taken out before the arrival of the guests of honor; therefore all the little ones outside, with their tiny bellies filled almost to bursting, were in place with a view. The larger ones watched through the windowpane that sometimes steamed up from the warmth of all the scrumptious food.

"Micah, you mind your manners inside the cabin." David's words were said with authority. "He is such a blessing to have around," Zipporah said as she gave her K-9 protector another treat. "Speaking of blessings," Zipporah smiled as she pointed toward the hand-washing sink. "Shall we wash before the blessing?" It was always the custom to wash one's hands before the blessing is said over the meal.

Outside the cabin the birds made a symphony for all to dance to. Mr. and Mrs. Turtledove waltzed across the hayfield with grace surpassed by none. The younger group led by the twins wanted faster music. Isaiah Bald Eagle took a place in the branches of the large maple tree while waiting and listening for God's Spirit to move. He would then share a Word in light of the occasion. Petra and Yael sat together. Between the two of them one could keep at least one eye on the twins.

The last day of Hanukkah was as precious as the first. It also started when Sabbath ended. This day was different. There are other farms in the area and sometimes Zipporah goes to visit with some of the believers who love and respect ADONAI. They must be great people because she always comes home happier than she left. There is also a special glow about her after she spends time with her people-friends.

Food seems to be second only to God at these events. This evening Zipporah made hummus from some chickpeas she had cooked up before the Sabbath. She enjoyed being in the kitchen. Worship music played in the background as she mixed the Israeli *tahini*, olive oil and juices and the right amount of herbs and spices along with olive bread for dipping, and other treats.

Her last act of the evening was to feed her little animal friends at the compost pile.

Petra Possum, David Bobcat and Isaiah Bald Eagle kept an eye out for trouble at all times. Security on the farm had to remain constant; the loss of a little one affects everyone. Momma alone keeps our *Dodi Haganah* on their toes. I don't know what would happen without our "Beloved Protectors."

Yosef was the first to fall asleep by the warmth of the fire. Tamar was proud of herself, having stayed awake later than her brother born only 5 seconds before her. "Momma, Yosef fell asleep," trying to hide her own yawn.

"I got this one." David ever so gently scooped the still sleeping chipmunk to his tiny nest.

"Come along young lady." Yael never skipped a beat when it came to the children. "Thank you David. I would have made him walk. Suppose a predator had been about. I saw Felix…"

"And so did I. Now stop being a mother long enough to get some sleep yourself. We have NOT lost a little one yet."

Pinky was still jumping up and down. "I'm not tired. Isaiah please read to us, then you can tell us a story, then you could pray for us."

"We can start now with prayer. I would ask you to lead but I think we would never get out if you did."

So everyone settled down for a wonderful end to a gracious evening on the farm.

Zipporah walked through the back yard on her way into the cabin. "Safety first," she said as she checked to make sure all was well. Some are safe in their little nest, hole, branch or whatever they call a bed. Still, others remained in the same spot where Zipporah had left them. That always amazed her. Whispers could barely be heard as she walked through the back door of the cabin.

"Did you smell that?" Pinky was the first to speak, of course. "She was on the other people's farm. There are sheep, chickens, and two different dogs. I think one was the big white dog we've seen."

"Too much!" David Bobcat interrupted, "You may bring on predators with your constant chatter."

"Let us bow our heads in silent prayer." Isaiah Bald Eagle came to the rescue with his unending words of wisdom.

So ended the Hanukkah season. Opening and closing with the Word of God and prayer. All were blessed.

Winter on the Farm

One of the most beautiful blessings Adonai has ever created is snow. Each snowflake individual, so unique only the creator, Himself, can tell them apart.

Zipporah caught her first glance out of the dining room window. Her heart filled with delight as she threw on her coat and boots, *Baruch haShem!* giving praises to the Name of the Lord. Turning on the outdoor light, she squeezed out of the door and down the back steps. She sat with her head back watching the snowfall as it reflected off the light. Tiny life forms, dancing down, leaving a glowing trail behind them.

Some snowflakes melted into droplets of water; others joined together to make the most picturesque scene. Everything from the highest mountain to the smallest of pebbles took refuge under the blanket of pure white snow. It was truly a sight to behold, bringing a feeling of peace and calm. A closeness to the Creator of all things. One can only be awestruck by such magnificence. The amount of snowflakes it takes to make a snowball alone is incredible.

Zipporah's thoughts wandered off to the chores she had to do in the morning before Sabbath. "Tomorrow has enough worries of its own," she said to herself. The temperature felt perfect. She sat back for one last glance before she went in for the night, thanking God for His goodness.

Snow is so important because it waters the ground for plants. Our wells also refill with the spring thaw.

Satisfied with her time with her Creator and His creation, Zipporah whispered *leila tov*. A "good night" to all.

Mornings are always joyful; the sound of worship music fills the cabin as Zipporah lifts her voice in praise. Praying, singing, dancing and Bible reading is all part of her daily routine.

Time slipped by so fast she hadn't realized, "I had better start cooking." She started peeling, grating, slicing, dicing, roasting and boiling. Before you knew it, the feast was ready.

As always Zipporah's last duty in the kitchen was to take out the compost. Blueberry, mango, orange, carrot, potato. The little animals had a buffet of yummy treats.

As Zipporah walked around the side of the cabin, she saw footprints. "Those are not one of friendly animal prints," she thought to herself. She followed the tracks that circled the cabin before going back inside. She did feel some concern so she whispered a short prayer and went back to work.

Zipporah was loading the food into the car when she noticed David Bobcat in deep conversation with Petra Possum and decided to see if she could get any answers as to the mysterious paw track in the snow.

"Zipporah." Petra was the first to speak. "We had trouble during the night." Petra was still upset over her run in with Felix.

"Petra is such a brave soul," David Bobcat announced. "She protected the smaller animals at the risk of her own life."

"It wasn't that bad, David," Petra said.

"You should have seen it, Zipporah," Pinky Skunk went on. "Petra let Felix Red Fox have it but good. She is our hero; Felix will not be back anytime soon. She….."

David jumped in at that point, "Petra stands on guard by the cabin while I patrol the perimeter of the property. Felix made his way to the compost where many of the smaller animals lived. He thought Petra would be no match for him; however, her military training came in very handy. The Israeli Defense Force would be very proud of her right now," he concluded as he patted her on the back.

"I saw the whole thing." Ezekiel Wise Owl spoke from the safety of a maple tree branch.

Felix came creeping, sniffing along until he came upon Petra, who had already spotted him and was going out to meet him. He didn't even see her until she was just a few yards away. Taken by surprise he looked up and called out her name. "Petra, you look good this evening." Petra continued to approach and he got aggressive and started licking his chops as if he were going to eat her. He even said what a yummy treat she would be and that is when Petra jumped through the air, one leg moving in a circular motion connected to the left side of Felix's face, turning his head almost completely around. Ezekiel was having far too much fun telling this story. "I thought he was done but he got up and ran away."

"You did not see fit to lend Petra a helping hand?" Zipporah knew she was putting Ezekiel on the spot but could not help herself.

"She was doing just fine on her own." Ezekiel's pride was somewhat hurt.

"Well, I'm proud of you, my dear," Zipporah said. "Job well done. Having you here has been a great load off my mind." She stooped over and gave Petra a little kiss on the cheek.

Petra blushed, saying, "It is an honor to live here with you all."

"I have to leave for the evening. Keep up the good work." Zipporah smiled as she spoke. "I will check back with you when I get home."

All was well that evening; however the morning was another story.

As Zipporah walked out of the back door, she saw a trail of turkey feathers. Puzzled, she looked around to see if she could find any clues.

Isaiah flew to Zipporah in order to break the news. Soon Mr. and Mrs. Turtle-dove appeared to pay their respects followed by Ezekiel, Methuselah accompanied by Mr. and Mrs. Squirrel. One by one all the animals came to pay honor to a fallen hero.

Pinky was the first to break the silence. "Zipporah it was awful," was all she could say, not even lifting her head to speak.

"Please tell me what happened." Zipporah was on the verge of tears, seeing everyone so sad.

A young coyote cub wandered onto the farm. The turkeys were preparing to fly up to the tree and roost for the night when he caught sight of them. He ran toward the flock as they scattered in different directions. The cub was in full chase of a young one. Thomas saw that the little guy could not outrun the coyote cub and was not yet very good at flying. Thomas ran toward the coyote cub to get his attention. Thomas gave his life so that young turkey could live.

No one spoke for a while. There weren't any words of comfort for a fallen friend.

"We know who is behind this." Ezekiel could no long stand such a loud silence.

"We will not assign blame for what ADONAI has given as instinct." Zipporah swallowed hard in order to speak. "We will mourn in a way that is biblical—cry together, laugh in his memory, and pray for comfort for our loss. Isaiah, please take it from here," was all she could say, as she walked through the yard to the back steps of the cabin.

Zipporah walked mindlessly through the cabin to the bay window where she could see, as well as be seen by all the animals. "Isaiah, please lead us in the 'Mourner's Kaddish.' "

Everyone's mind wandered to a special moment in time with Thomas. Gideon smiled good-naturedly as he thought about the time Thomas was escorting the flock through a field where Gideon was having a midday snack. Of course, Thomas bravely protecting the flock from a perceived threat began kicking Gideon until he heard innocent Gideon yelling for help. He had to hold back his laughter at the thought of the look on Thomas' face when he realized Gideon meant no harm. Zipporah's mind went back to all the times she watched Thomas lead the flock across the hay field, never loosing even one.

Even Micah, our brave K-9, came to pay his respects. "Good bye, my friend and fallen hero." Micah's voice carried throughout the valley. Micah did not shout, he simply spoke with authority. "You will be remembered." Attached to his collar was a pouch of his most treasured possessions, dog tags from other fallen heroes. A wild turkey doesn't have dog tags; therefore memories will keep Thomas alive in his heart.

The flock was inconsolable. Females and little ones alike swallowed their grief. The other males in the flock did not want to talk about what everyone was thinking: who would lead the flock? He would have to be strong and brave, yet humble.

Then, together, they all said the Mourner's Kaddish, a praise to God said when someone dies.

"Amein." Zipporah looked around for the faces that went with the choir of voices she had not heard before.

"Shalom, are you here to pay your respects to our fallen hero?" Zipporah welcomed the group.

"Yes, we are. I am Luke Rabbit, the eldest. These are my brothers, Simon and Mark. We live by the church across the street. We had to leave our women and children in a safe place.

"We are afraid Felix Red Fox may have led that young coyote cub right to us.

"We must give up the home we have loved for so many years. Now that we are halfway through the winter, we must search farther out for food. The young ones will not be safe until after the spring thaw. We have heard of Zipporah's Farm. We know of the strength in your unity. We also love Adonai and would like to join you here on the farm."

The atmosphere went from one of mourning to the celebration of a new tribe joining the farm.

David Bobcat, Hal Horse and Petra Possum escorted the "Honorable Rabbit Brothers" back to their families in order to bring them all back safely.

Of course, all the farm animals followed along hoping to get their first glimpse of the Rabbit Tribe. Some have seen them before in their wanderings, others who never wandered jumped up and down happily.

Knowing she would soon have a bunch of hungry rabbits on her hands, Zipporah got all the compost together and took it out for her new fluffy friends. "Yael, you had better mind your manners. Remember to be kind." She reached out her hand to pat Yael on the head but she is so tiny Zipporah's large hand covered Yael from head to tail.

Zipporah's heart went out to the Rabbit Tribe as she saw David and Hal carrying the family members who were too weak from hunger or who had been wounded running in a chase. The sight of this charitable act of kindness bought tears to Zipporah's eyes. Petra helped an elderly female, while Gideon chatted in his friendly way with some of the young males. Finally Zipporah knew they had reached the end of the line when she heard Pinky, "You are going to love it here. Everyone is so loving. Would you like to see where I live? Would you like to come to my home after you eat?"

"Welcome all." Zipporah did not like to interrupt anyone; however, Pinky can go on and on.

"I am sure you are all hungry and tired. Please eat to your satisfaction, then you may begin looking for a suitable place to make your home." Zipporah was so filled with love and joy as she looked at all the white, black, brown, black and white, brown and white, black and brown rabbits.

Zipporah excused herself, giving David, Hal and Petra little nods. As they whispered in a huddle, Zipporah suggested the next course of action. "David, have Isaiah gather all his birds of prey. Meet me at the northeast border of the farm at noon. Petra, please help the rabbit families get settled."

"Hal, I need to ride on your back to get up high and look about." Hal bent over to give Zipporah an assist. "What is your plan?" Hal is noble and speaks with dignity.

"First we will go to the packs and let them know we will not stand for any of our animals being eaten. Then we will go to Fox Forest and confront Felix. He is the one who led that cub to the farm. We will live in peace together." They knew Zipporah meant business.

The air felt as it did just before a snowstorm, not at all cold. Or was it fury that made Zipporah feel hot as she rode on Hal's back. Leading a small army of a host of different animals, some out for blood, others heeding Zipporah's words of peace, still others not sure if they could control themselves, even if they wanted to. Years of fear and loss had reached their height of terror, accompanied with somewhat of a release of all those suppressed emotions. Running on adrenalin, the smaller animals lagged behind. Their little legs stretched to the limit in a futile attempt to keep up.

After the better part of an hour, David's faithful nose led the army through coyote territory right to a solitary coyote cub. Terrified, he looked up with round, warm, brown eyes, without lifting his head. The words would barely be heard as he spoke, "I was only doing what I was taught. I wanted to make my Momma proud of me." A lonely tear escaped from one of his eyes.

"Vengeance is mine," says ADONAI. Zipporah, feeling compassion for the frightened cub, reminded everyone, "We are not here for revenge."

She went on to tell the coyote cub that the farm was off limits to hunters, predators, or anyone else seeking to harm, steal, or destroy.

"Do you understand me?" she asked the cub.

"I think so." The cub felt a lot more relaxed knowing he was not going to be a snack. "You do not want us on your farm."

"Let's eat him!" came a yell from the crowd followed by others.

"We should drag him back to Thomas' family!"

"Let's barbeque him!"

"Yeah, Yummy!"

"Enough! What is wrong with you? Most of you are vegetarian; how could you say such things? Look at him. He is more afraid of us then we are of him. He has been abandoned to be eaten. We shall not punish him for acting on instinct and survival skills. We will teach him our ways and let him chose."

"What is your name?" Zipporah's voice softened.

"Y'hoshua."

"Y'hoshua, do you understand what a vegetarian is?"

"Yes, they are the animals that eat vegetables and we eat them. Vegetarians taste the best."

"Get him!!!!!!!!"

"We are not going to stand for this!" The shouts from the crowd started again.

"The only thing we are not going to stand for are vicious words; can you not see he is a baby. He is no older than the twins, Tamar and Yosef.

"Miss Zipporah," Y'hoshua sounded so humble and polite, "May I visit your farm? I promise never to hurt any farm animals, only protect them as you have protected me."

"Do you know and love Adonai?" She needed to be sure of his relationship with the Creator.

"I never heard of this Adonai before," Y'hoshua answered honestly.

"I will send Isaiah Bald Eagle to teach you. When Isaiah tells me you are not a threat and you accept Adonai and the ways of Torah and the *B'rit Hadashah*, the New Covenant, only then will you become family."

"Where will I find Mr. Bald eagle?"

"He will find you. Classes will start soon."

With that, they were off to Fox Forest.

It did not take long to find Felix. Flat on his stomach, dragging his injured left hind leg. "It wasn't me, I tell you. It was the coyote cub. He did it. Look what he did to my leg. He got me just as I was jumping into my hole. The pain is unbearable."

"Let us help you." David Bobcat approached Felix. "I can put an instant end to your pain."

"David whatever do you mean?" Felix used his sly smile to hide his fear.

"You led that young innocent cub to the farm. The coyotes know better than to bring him anywhere near us."

"Now David, you couldn't possibly blame me for the actions of a whole different species."

"That poor little guy is now abandoned, left to fend for himself. He may not even make it through the night."

"Is that so? Is the poor thing hurt?"

"Felix, you are shameful," David's instincts kicked in. "The only reason I will not eat you here on the spot is because I do not want to traumatize the vegetarian animals."

"Oh, those little guys would never get over the shock of such a sight." Felix was trembling with fear at this point. "Y'hoshua is alone and hungry." David toyed with him a while. "Who?" Felix cowered as he asked. "Y'hoshua, you know, that coyote cub you were referring to."

At this point Felix was so filled with terror that he could not even speak. "Well um, I um, well he…"

Zipporah could no longer control her laughter, "I think he has had enough."

"Are you sure Zipporah? Since he is wounded I would be more than happy to carry him to the cub."

"That will not be necessary. That is, of course, if Felix can't take the pain, and look at all the blood he has lost. That is bound to attract predators. We may as well let the little cutie eat." Zipporah couldn't help herself. Felix needed to learn a good lesson.

"Little cutie?! When did he go from predator to little cutie? Just look at what he did to my leg. What is going on around here? He is the problem, not me. I've never hurt even one of your precious little animals."

A sudden roaring-like sound came from David, getting everyone's attention. "You watch how you speak to Zipporah or you will never recover from the trauma you get from me!"

"Stand down, David, he looks like he is ready to have a heart attack." Zipporah spoke firmly but softly at this point.

Felix put his right hand against the left side of his chest. "David, Please, I can't take much more of this stress."

"Stress!!!" David was furious, "Do you want to know what real stress is? I have had enough of you." David approached with his mouth open.

Zipporah dismounted Hal and stood between David and Felix. "What has gotten into you?" She never needed to tell David anything more than once before this event. "He has learned his lesson."

With that she turned and yelled for all to hear, "Time to go home and live in peace and safety."

The heartfelt welcome the host of animals received was wondrous.

"We picked up a few more animals seeking shelter and protection during the winter." Zipporah thought very highly of Petra Possum and knew Petra could be trusted with any task. "Would you mind helping them get settled when you're finished with the Rabbit tribe?"

"They are all settled." Petra was happy to announce the task had already been completed. "They are very dependent on each other, but as a group they stay to themselves."

Petra continued, "Now that I am all done with them I'll start helping others who want assistance."

"I don't know how I ever got along without you. You have become such a leader among us." Petra could only smile shyly, dropping her head to hide her blushing cheeks as she rocked back and forth. "I love it here," was all Petra could say. "We love you more than you could ever know." Zipporah hugged her bravest of soldiers, gave her a kiss on the cheek, then set her tiny possum friend back on the ground and watched her take off, following orders.

David apologized to Zipporah for losing his temper.

"David," Zipporah spoke lovingly and reassuringly, "You are a great warrior and a defender of the weak. You need not ever be sorry for who you are. Stand tall, be seen. Many depend on you for security and charity, to which, you give generously."

"Thank you for your kind words." David spoke in a gentle and humble manner for such a strong and respected animal. "Is there anything else I can do for you this evening"? David wanted to help get everyone settled.

That evening the bon-fire flames danced in ever changing colors warming the souls and bodies of one big happy family under the starlit sky.

Isaiah Bald Eagle shared God's Word ending in a time a prayer and welcome for all newcomers to Zipporah's farm, along with the reassurance that they will never need to weather a storm alone again.

"You are all *mishpocha* now and as "family" you will be cared for and protected as long as you obey Adonai, Torah and the rules." Isaiah liked to put Adonai first. "It is so important that we understand GOD's Word. If anyone has any questions, I am always here for you. You are not alone!"

Winter went on for another six weeks but there was never want on the farm. God provided enough for everyone. Good food, clean air and water. In the spring the land will be ready to begin the new season. Until then, everyone on the farm will huddle together for warmth and await spring's new beginning.

Growing on the Farm

Trees, saplings, bushes, vines, shrubs, plants…the list goes on. There are also parts like branches, limbs, trunks, bark, leaves, sap, roots, bulbs, seeds…

Next we can talk about the types—maple, pine, elm, birch, hickory, dog, fruit bearing, flowering…

Indoor plants, outdoor plants, cactus, creeping plants, hanging plants… There is no end.

Some parts are delicate, look, smell and feel good. Other parts are workers and feeders that may not feel, smell or taste good at all. However, bugs, birds and animals of varying sizes make their homes and fill their tiny bellies by these things.

First let's talk about chlorophyll, the green part, whose job is photosynthesis. This process uses radiant energy from the sun and water, takes carbon dioxide, which people breathe out, and turns it into oxygen, which people need to breathe to live. People need plant life to live and plant life needs people to live. Both need food, sun and water.

Then there is the sap. Maple and sugar are wonderful sweeteners; others can be used as medicine.

Some tree barks can also be used for healing. Bark is most loved by insects, birds and animals with horns. Different microscopic bugs spend their days eating leaves, sap, bark and god-only-knows what else, to their hearts delight. Birds eat the bugs, and use twigs, leaves, vines and whatever else they can find that is useful to make their nests.

From the simplest of creatures to the greatest, all animals need trees in some way or another.

Trees also need to be pruned. Leaves, branches, vines and such, sometimes get sick, just as people sometimes get sick. Sometimes there is something you can give to the plant to make it better. So when the plant uses more energy and resources to keep alive certain parts, the plant, itself, will hold back nutrients to the sick part and allow it to dry up and fall off on its own. In almost the same way God takes things out of our lives that are not good for us. The Bible tells us in *The Parable of the wheat and tares,* "Any tree that does not bear fruit will be cast out and then thrown into the fire."

Yael Chipmunk makes her home with the twins in a hollow log but has food hoarded in many different trees around the farm. Isaiah Bald Eagle made his nest in the tallest tree on the highest mountain top, where he can keep a diligent eye on the farm. Rahab and Barry Bluebird make their home in a sturdy maple tree, while Hadassah and Caleb Chickadee prefer a lovely scented dogwood tree. Sammy and Abby Crow are so hidden no one really knows where there live. Mr. and Mrs. Turtle-Dove have the most exquisite estate, glamorous, yet tasteful. Mr. and Mrs. Squirrel have an equally large but more functional home with many rooms for storage. They even have a handsome suite for their welcomed guess, Methuselah Grey Squirrel.

Deer bucks rub their horns on the bark and bear just love a nice back scratching on a tree trunk. Anyone lost in the woods could find their way home using the moss that grows on the north side of a tree.

Squirrels and chipmunks, and different animals, run circles around trees, branches, vines, even twigs. Forests are playgrounds to animals. Some animals sit in trees and groom themselves and each other.

Turkeys only go home at night to sleep. They don't always sleep in the same tree but move about from night to night. The trees haven't got a clue as to where the turkeys will sleep on any given night.

When spring arrives and the trees begin to bloom they each give off a unique scent. The colors are so diverse that there aren't names for all them. And the shade is so wonderful in the summer. Many marriage proposals, birth announcements, and news of all types have been shared under the shades of trees.

Children just loves tree houses and tree swings. Climbing trees, running around trees, swinging from tree branches. We not only get beautiful and sweet scented flowers from trees, we also get delicious fruit like apples, oranges, and cherries. Then there are bushes like blueberry, elderberry, and raspberry and nuts like pecan, hazel, and cashew. A bounty of wonderful treats.

"Boker tov, Abba." Zipporah whispered good morning to her Heavenly Daddy as she opened her eyes for the first time that morning. Still half asleep, she took in the full view of the newly fallen blanket of pure white snow, attempting to take in all of God's glory through His creation. The way the snow can completely cover every branch and trunk of all the trees. The mountain trees are so covered that the mountains themselves look like one big snow ball.

As Zipporah's eyes scan the hayfield, she noticed something she hadn't seen before—a line in the snow. She jumped out of bed and threw open the window. Her heart stopped for a moment as she realized the red line before her appeared to be blood. She put on her coat and boots ran outside.

Zipporah was taken by surprise at what was found. Red body, black framing a white face, so perfectly blended to form the cutest little critter. Less than a year old, weak and wounded, this handsome young fox half walked and half crawled from Fox Forest. "I seek asylum," was all he had the strength to say.

Immediately the Ruach filled Zipporah with love and compassion. She cradled the little guy in her arms as she carried him to the back steps. "You are welcome here. What is your name?"

"Ruben," he replied looking up at her with the biggest, saddest eyes she had ever seen in all of her days.

Zipporah swallowed, hardly able to speak, "This farm is your new home. You are safe now." Fighting tears Zipporah wanted to be strong for her new ward.

Ruben fought excruciating pain as he recounted the tragic event of that night. "I was so hungry. Momma had gone hunting days ago and hadn't come back. I was afraid I may be an…" His voice trailed off until it was barely audible, "orphan."

"There are no orphans on our farm." Zipporah, no longer fighting tears, allowed them to flow freely. "Is this the first time your Momma has been gone this long?"

"No."

"Well, there you go." Zipporah tried to turn things around, "You stay. I will tend to your wounds, then you will eat something."

Gently rubbing oil into his wounds, Zipporah prayed to ADONAI, "Please heal this broken child, *ba-shem*, "in the name of," Yeshua. Amen"

Ruben's voice was weak, "My Uncle Felix was eating his catch. Being family, I assumed he would let me have a few bites. I was wrong. He made an example of me."

Zipporah's body shook violently as she cried uncontrollably. "I'm so sorry that happened to you. I assure you of this, Felix will never touch you again."

Finished, holding Ruben in one arm, using the other to put some hay into an empty box, she made a cozy little bed. "Make yourself nice and comfy; I will return with food and a blanket."

She returned quickly with the promised covering and a bowl of berries, nut, and cheese. "Now you eat and stay in bed. I will check on you after I take Hal for a ride." She went into the back, stopping only to get a few carrots and an apple for Hal Horse before running out of the front door.

"Good morning Handsome Hal," Zipporah sang as she walked into the barn. I have breakfast for you."

"A bit early, isn't it?" Hal noticed his oat bowl was still full.

"Are you up for a ride this morning?"

"This and every morning!" Hal was always happy to carry Zipporah on his back; however he did notice that she wasn't her peppy self this morning. She hung her head as she fed the carrots to Hal one by one. "Might this ride have anything to do with your sad face?

"Nothing gets past you, my old friend." She tried to smile but only half achieved her goal. "My heart is heavy. We will ride and sing praises to ADONAI, which always fixes thing."

Zipporah lovingly brushed Hal's shiny coat before she gently saddled him up. Hal bowed, Zipporah jumped up and they were off.

"Where to?"

"Fox Forest."

"That explains a lot. What has Felix done?"

"I would rather not talk about it. You will see later"

When they came upon Felix he was sleeping with what appeared to be a big grin on his face. Hal placed his hoof gently on Felix's chest and very slowly applied pressure until Felix woke up.

"What?" Felix had no idea why they were there.

"How dare you hurt that poor little fox?" Zipporah didn't even try to hide her fury.

"Is that what this is about? What did he say?"

"I saw him. He didn't need to say much"

"So why are you here?" Felix did not know what he had done wrong.

"We are here to put an end to your brutality."

"What do you mean?" Felix is getting really nervous at this point.

"Y'hoshua is your family. You should be trying to help him, not hurt him."

"That brat. He is my sister's responsibility, not mine."

"So, you do not know how to share," Hal asked. Hal was puzzled by Felix's selfishness. Sharing is all Hal knew. "How could you not give the little guy a portion?"

"Why should I, as I said he is my sister's brat, not mine." Felix's arrogance infuriated Hal and he put more pressure on Felix's chest in an attempt to frighten him.

"Felix!" Zipporah spoke firmly, "You are never to step foot on my farm again. You are not welcome. We do NOT want you there. I have protected you long enough. Now you must fend for yourself."

"But...but." Felix could not find the words to say.

"But nothing." Hal knew when Zipporah spoke she meant what she said. "There is no more to be said. We will be watching out for you."

"Let's go Hal, I do not want to even look at him anymore."

By the time Hal carried Zipporah back to the farm news of the new family had spread.

"Can we see him?" Gideon asked?

"How do you know it is him? It could be her." Pinky was hopeful.

"His name is Y'hoshua." Zipporah was amused by the two. "He is not well; you may see him when he is better.

And he did get better. He grew up to be wiser and stronger than his uncle Felix. Everyone loved Y'hoshua. Y'hoshua especially liked Petra Possum. He had heard that she was fearless and even got the better of Felix.

So, life goes on. Everyone patiently awaiting spring, especially the trees.

Spring on the Farm

Spring had finally arrived. The birds that had flown south for the winter were now returning. The trees were starting to bud. Life was returning to the farm. The smells of spring filled the air. It was time to get busy.

The ground has to be tilled and conditioned before seeds could be planted. Timing is everything. Planting too soon, before a frost, and the plants will not survive. Waiting too long and the plants will not have enough time to grow to maturity.

Rain is essential to the health, growth and maintenance of plants. If we do not get enough rain, the crops will dry up and die. If we get too much, the crops will be washed of the nutrients they need to live and grow, making them wilt. Only God can give rain. His Word says He gives rain to the just and the unjust. He gives "latter rain" and "former rain." Both are needed to wet and soften the ground enough to turn over the soil in order to loosen it enough for the plant's roots to grow deep.

Some flowers like tulips, daffodils, and lilies grow not from seeds, but from bulbs. The ones that regrow every year are called "perennials." Some grow one year and do not regrow the next year. These are called "annuals," because they have to be planted every year, annually.

Zipporah was planting sunflowers seeds when she noticed Petra Possum approaching another possum. She has never seen this elderly looking possum before and decides to go investigate.

"Howdy, young lady," Zipporah heard him say.

Petra was not sure what to make of this one, so she was polite but kept her guard up. "Shalom," she replied.

"You sure are pretty," he said with a smile.

"Thank you." Petra wanted to be polite yet firm. "Where did you come from?" she asked.

"Yonder farm" he replied

"I've never heard of 'Yonder farm,'" Petra clearly confused.

"Yonder, about a mile. Y'all gotta go down the road, around the mountain and through the woods." He used his hands to show directions.

"Okay," she listened patiently.

"You got anything to eat round here?"

"Sure." she led him to the compost pile.

"We gotta leave our farm on account of this new puppy won't let us be."

Petra even more confused, "Won't let you be what?"

Now the old possum was confused, "What?"

"What will this puppy not allow you to be?" She was really trying to understand this old country possum.

"Young lady, what is you talkin' 'bout?"

"Sir, I really am trying to understand you."

"Ain't I talkin' English?" Now the old possum was growing impatient.

"Not like I've ever heard," Petra replied.

"Father, are you bothering this young lady?"

Petra turned and locked eyes with the most handsome possum she had ever seen.

For a while no one said a word. Both were unable to speak. Finally Petra came to her senses.

"And who might the two of you be?"

"Sir?" No response, "Sir? Are you hard of hearing? Can you hear what I am saying?"

"Solo is you ok" the father asked his son. "We call him Solo because he is the only child my beloved late wife gave me."

Petra didn't know what to say, "I'm sorry to hear that."

"It is okay; I don't need no more mouths to feed," the old possum replied.

"I was referring to your wife." Petra had enough of this conversion. She started to walk away when she heard his voice.

"Dr. Solomon Possum at your service." He was absolutely taken by her beauty. "This is my father, Steven."

"Wonderful, we can use a doctor on the farm." Petra showed a bit more excitement than she had intended.

"Not a medical doctor," Solomon announced, "a Ph.D."

"Oh," was all she dared to say, not wanting to appear too interested.

"Ph.D in agriculture and horticulture." Solomon's smile took Petra's breath away.

“That school ruined him,” Steven said. “Was s’posed to be a farmer like his Pa. Now he wanna do everything different. Children just ain’t what they used to be.”

The young possum was well dressed and obviously educated, in contrast to his elderly father in overalls.

“Please help yourself to our compost pile.” Petra turned and pointed to the goodies.

Solo could not allow her to just walk away; he may never see her again. “Please join us for a bite to eat.”

Although Petra wasn’t hungry she thought she would seize the moment. “Of course. I would be happy to show you around when we’re done.”

Zipporah was watching and found the whole thing amusing. She knew love at first sight when she saw it. Her heart was so filled with joy at the thought of Petra and Solomon staring at each other with stars in their eyes.

For as long as Petra had been on the farm, she was always a caretaker and protector. She thought of others before herself. Petra is, by far, the most loving and unselfish animal that Zipporah had ever known. It was about time someone came along who would love and care for her

“Tell me about you,” Solomon said as he sat next to her. He no longer felt hungry. Petra smiled. No one had ever asked her about herself before and she was at a loss for words. “There really isn’t much to tell. I’ve lived on Zipporah’s Farm for some time now.”

“Who is Zipporah?” Steven possum asked.

"Well, she is the most loving and kindest person I have ever met." Petra became very animated when she spoke of her favorite person.

"Father, you are getting us off the subject." Solomon tried not to sound too annoyed.

"See, that is what I mean. I always been "Pa." He comes back from that school and now I'm "father." Steven said the word "father," sarcastically. "You done spent too much time with those uppity folk. You need to remember where you come from."

"Evidently, I remembered how to get home because I am here, aren't I?"

"Yeah, and ain't you the smarty pants?" Steven did not care to carry on this conversation any longer. "Just hush up and eat."

Petra, being a peaceful possum, did not enjoy the quarrel. "I had better get going. It has been nice meeting the two of you." With that she turned to walk away.

"Wait!" Solomon could not allow her to leave on that note. "I will take you up on your offer of that tour now. Pa, I will catch up with you later."

"Yeah, yeah, yeah." Steven didn't even try to hide his annoyance.

With that Petra and Solomon started the stroll that would bond them together for life. Solomon wanted to tell Petra how beautiful she was. He wanted to take her hand and dance around the hayfield.

Petra, on the other hand, felt light-headed, her mind going in so many different directions that she couldn't think straight. "What is wrong with you?" she asked herself. "Get a grip," she told herself.

Solomon wanted to know all there was to know about this elegant possum.

Just as he was about to speak he was interrupted by shouts from Saul Squirrel.

"Help! It's happening. It's coming."

Petra was brought back to reality. "What is it Saul? What's happening?"

"The baby is coming. Quick, get Zipporah." Saul was frantic.

"We can handle this."

Petra jumped into action. "It is a natural thing. The females of every species have been giving birth since the Creation. Take me to her."

Petra arrived just in time to assist Dvora with the birth of her little one. "I'm here sweetie; we can do this together." Petra had never delivered a baby before but thought she had better at least appear to be confident. She whispered a prayer and prepared to catch. "Relax and breath" Petra urged.

Dvora forgot her pain long enough to yell at Petra, "Together? And just how much of this pain are you going to take? Oh yes, you are going to do the relax part."

At this point Petra knew she had bitten off more than she could chew. "Dvora, you need to push," she instructed.

Saul hadn't even noticed Solomon standing there until he spoke. "She is quite a lady," Solomon announced, still feeling love struck.

"Yes she is. This is our first baby," Saul said.

Solomon didn't have the heart to tell Saul he had been referring to Petra and just went with the moment. "Congratulations!"

Suddenly they heard one last scream, the cry of a tiny newborn squirrel.

Shock went through Saul. "My baby, that's my baby."

He almost knocked Petra over as he ran past her, "Honey, are you okay?" He was frantic at this point.

"It's a girl." Dvora handed Saul the fruit of their love. "What shall we name her? How about Ruth, after your mother?"

"I have never loved anyone as much as I love you at this very moment." Saul being overwhelmed with emotion, tears falling from his eyes, bent over and gave his beloved a kiss on her forehead.

"I love you too, my husband." Now that the whole ordeal was over Dvora had returned to her sweet self.

Methuselah Squirrel was beside himself, overcome with more joy than he had ever known in his life. "May I stand in as acting grandfather?"

"You are our family. We would love for you to be little Ruthie's 'grandfather.'"

Methuselah was so happy to think he had become a grandparent to the child of his friends turned family.

The atmosphere on the farm was that of love and joy. A new life was born onto the farm. Ruth Rahab Squirrel is the cutest little thing. The twins, Tamar and Josef were glad they were no longer the youngest animals on the farm and couldn't wait to meet their new family member. Everyone came from near and far to see the baby, bringing gifts.

Mr. and Mrs. Turtle-Dove showered mother and baby with various nuts.

Mr. and Mrs. Blue Jay shared their seeds.

The crows weaved blankets for the little one.

The Rabbit Clan got together and picked a mountain of grass for the family to munch on.

The Turkey Flock gleaned corn and the Hens, Barley.

Everyone gave generously. Even the twins brought a mango pit from the compost pile.

Zipporah made it her business to see that the celebration was a feast for the eyes as well as the belly. Flowers everywhere and food in abundance. Music and dancing. Everyone giving thanks to Adonai for the new life. Mr. and Mrs. Squirrel were humbled by such great love that they received, proudly showing off the little bundle of joy.

Gideon and Y'hoshua, now the best of friends, played happily together, the twins running around with great energy. Laughter filled the air.

Solomon was amazed that so many different animals lived together so peacefully, "Is it always like this around here?" he asked Petra.

"Well, there is never a lack of love. We face hard times just like anyone else; the only difference is that we face things together. We function as a family. All for one and one for all!" Petra proclaimed. "Everyone has a unique gift. No one is ever left out of anything."

Solomon looked Petra directly in the eyes as he spoke, stating, "You are so beautiful." Solomon finally got up the nerve to say what he had been thinking since the moment he saw her. "I have never had any interest in ladies before. All I cared about was books and learning, however, you have captivated me. I cannot get you off my mind. I want to know all there is to know about you."

"Well," Petra said, "I was born on a ship. I spent most of my life in Netanya, Israel before I decided I wanted to see more of the world."

She paused for just a moment and Solomon took that opportunity to jump in. "You do not understand what I am saying." He got down on one knee and took her hand. "Petra, until now I never knew what love was but now I'm sure." He hesitated for a second before he spoke again. "Petra I love you. Would you do me the honor of being my mate?"

Petra tried to speak but the words wouldn't travel from her brain to her mouth.

"I will be good to you," Solomon assured her. "I will take care of you. I promise to love you all the days of my life."

"I think I love you also," Petra finally admitted to herself as well as to Solomon. "However you do know I have responsibilities on the farm."

"Yes, I understand. I want to support you and take on responsibilities of my own. After all, I do have a Ph.D in agriculture and horticulture. I cannot think of a better place to put my education to work."

Petra could no longer remain silent. "Yes," was all she could manage to say.

"Yes?" Solomon jumped to his feet. "Yes!" he danced around. "She said yes!"

Petra suddenly felt very shy. "When you say, "mate" am I correct in assuming you mean marriage? *Huppah*, Rabbi, the whole ceremony?"

"Of course, *dodi*, my love. Nothing is too good for you." Solomon assumed Petra understood that is what he meant. "We are children of ADONAI and as such must always do what is right"

Now Petra was the one jumping and dancing.

Solomon and Petra decided not to make their announcement until after the baby shower, not wanting to take away from Mr. and Mrs. Squirrel's special occasion.

By sunset everyone had eaten to their hearts delight and was now enjoying Isaiah Bald Eagle's sermon. "Behold, children are a heritage from ADONAI. The fruit of the womb is a reward. Like arrows in the hand of a warrior. Blessed is the man who has his quiver full of them."

Hearts were melting at the thought of little Ruthie and the joy that she would bring to the farm. Everyone knows how precious life is. Even David Bob Cat let his guard down and got caught up in the moment. Ezekiel Wise Owl sat in his tree, almost smiling as he grumbled something about crumb snatchers.

Zipporah sat and watched, listening intently. Overjoyed at the thought of how she loved all those animals.

Petra and Solomon talked all night, not realizing how much time had passed until the sun came up. "By far that is the most beautiful sunrise I have ever seen," Solomon told Petra. "I believe it is all thanks to you. Everything has changed: the flowers smell sweeter, the food tastes better and I am happier than I have ever been."

"I agree," Petra responded. "However, we really should call it a night. I go on duty at noon."

"May I walk you home?" Solomon did not want to leave her side.

"Of course." Petra was thankful for every moment she shared with her new love.

On her way to Zipporah's cabin Petra practiced what she would say to Zipporah and hoped she would approve of her and Solomon.

Zipporah saw Petra coming and met her half way.

"I have something I would like to let you know." Petra searched for the right words. "It is really important to me that you understand."

"Please, speak freely, you know I respect you."

"Well," Petra began, "I...we wanted you to be the first to know." She hesitated for a moment. "It is just that..."

Zipporah almost knew what was coming. "Does this have anything to do with that handsome possum you've been spending so much time with?"

Now Petra was getting nervous. "Well. You see, we have been talking."

"Yes, I know." Zipporah spoke softly, hoping to encourage Petra.

"We were hoping you would allow us to..." Petra could not believe her own words, "We would like our wedding to be on the farm." She was finally about to finish her sentence.

"That would make me so happy," Zipporah exclaimed. "I think you and Solomon were made for each other. I will do all I can to make it my business to see that you have the best wedding ever."

"So, you approve!" Petra felt relieved.

"My dear, it is not for me to approve or disapprove," Zipporah said as she stroked Petra's cheek. "If you love each other, of course, you should get married and with the farm being your home, I cannot think of a better place for the two of you to share your wedding vows."

"Thank you!" Petra jumped into Zipporah's arms and gave her a great big hug. "I'm so happy. I have never been in love before. Solomon is great. He is kind and gentle and knowledgeable, and he can help on the farm. I cannot wait for you to meet him."

Zipporah could hardly speak, she was laughing so hard. "I have never heard you talk so much before. You must truly be in love. Shall we begin planning the wedding?"

"Oh yes, please." Petra was thrilled.

When the day had arrived, the whole farm was decorated with the most beautiful shades of lavender, violet and green. Wedding bells could be heard for miles away, calling all to attendance. Fruit, nuts, seeds and greens were abundant. Zipporah made all kinds of special treats for this joyous occasion.

Of course, Isaiah Bald Eagle said the blessing over the couple as they stood under the *huppah* before God and all creation, exchanging vows. After Petra walked around Solomon seven times and Solomon smashed the tiny glass with his foot, the couple was declared "husband and wife." So began their life together.

Yes, spring is a time of new beginnings on the farm. From births to marriages. Love grows and flows freely. All living together in harmony. Adonai in everyone's heart.